Are you happy with your life right now? Do you have everything that you really want? Your habits define you as a person and they are responsible for all the things that you have and do not have in your life right now. You may not realize this but it is true.

With this powerful guide you will be able to break those bad habits which are not supporting the life that you want and form new habits that will empower you to make a positive change. It is not going to be an easy journey as breaking habits you have had for a long time is going to be tough. Forming new habits is challenging as well.

But you must examine your habits and make the necessary changes if you want to truly succeed. To help you to do this we recommend that you create a strong reason or "why" you want to change your habits. Write this down and refer to it if your motivation drops.

We will explain in this guide how habits work and how they are formed. It is essential that you understand this to make the changes that you desire. We will explain the 3 R's neurological loop and the time that it takes to make changes to habits. There is also a section on habit formation phases which you must read.

Even when your new habit is automatic and you have successfully navigated all of the formation phases there will still be a chance that you could break a new good habit. So we have provided some proven ways for you to reinforce new habits that are simple and effective.

Getting rid of your bad habits will totally liberate you. It is a great feeling to change something that has been holding you back for a long time. Forming new empowering habits will also be a great experience for you and will make you feel confident about the future.

We suggest that you treat the breaking of your bad habits and the formation of your new good habits as an exciting journey. There will be a mixture of highs and lows throughout your journey and you need to know how to handle the low points. This is all covered in the guide so let's get started.

WHY YOU NEED TO BREAK BAD HABITS

You know that some habits are bad for you immediately don't you? Smoking cigarettes and drinking a lot of alcohol are two that instantly come to mind. Then there are bad eating habits such as regularly eating junk food. But not all of our bad habits are immediately obvious to us.

Some bad habits can be holding you back without you even realizing it. If you set goals for yourself (which you certainly should) to improve your life it is possible that some of your bad habits are preventing you from achieving your goals.

Your Choices can have a Dramatic Effect on your Life

As we continue our journey through life we make decisions all of the time. Most of these will be small decisions that we make without any thought but some of the decisions that we make can dramatically change the course of our life. Sometimes these decisions have a positive impact on our lives and sometimes a negative one.

These small decisions that we make on a regular basis can quickly form habits. We are creatures of routine and before you know it a new habit can form that takes us down the wrong road. Over the years you will have formed many habits both good and bad.

Developing Bad Habits to Escape from Reality

A lot of people form bad habits to escape from reality. An example of this is to spend a lot of time on social media rather than doing other things that you know you should be doing. Watching meaningless television is another example.

Another example is comfort eating. When some people get stressed out they reach for a large bag of chips or a candy bar for comfort. They know that eating these things are bad for them but it helps them to relax and relieve the pressure of the stress. Before they know it this becomes a bad habit and they are piling on the pounds!

Procrastination is a bad habit that so many people have. They put off doing things and they either get done in a rush at the last minute or they never get done at all. The more that people procrastinate the stronger the habit becomes.

Some bad habits are worse than others. What might seem a harmless habit initially can escalate into negative behavior such as constantly lying and leading a life of deceit. People can become so embroiled in these habits that cannot see how this is harming their life and preventing them from getting what they want.

Breaking Bad Habits can Save you Time

Time is a very precious resource and you can never get it back. Do you have any bad habits that lead you to waste a lot of your time? How about those hours that you spend on Facebook every day? Or that habit of perfectionism that you have which makes you go over things again and again until you believe that they are perfect?

A lot of people take time for granted. There is always tomorrow or next week right? Well hopefully that is true. But think about how much time you are currently wasting with bad habits. What else could you do with that precious time?

A common complaint these days is that people never have enough time to do all of the things that they want to do. For some this would change significantly if they broke the bad habits that steal their time.

Bad Habits can Negatively Impact your Relationships

Humans are social by nature but some bad habits can prevent you from forming the relationships that you really want. At the extreme end of the scale are addictions such as alcohol and drugs. These can seriously impact your career and personal relationships.

But other bad habits can prevent you from forming the right relationships as well. If you are a procrastinator then this is going to hold you back in your career. It could also prevent you from crating new friendships and also finding the perfect soul mate.

If you have a negativity habit and are always complaining about everything then this will drive a lot of people away that could be good friends and help you in your life. People tend to be much more attracted to positive people. Negative people only seem to attract other negative people which never moves them forward.

Bad Habits can Prevent you from achieving your Goals

Having a few bad habits can seriously limit you when it comes to achieving worthwhile goals in your life. A lot of people hit the bars on a Friday night with their friends and get pretty drunk. It doesn't matter what age you are the effects of alcohol will leave their mark. The next day you will feel lethargic and not want to do much at all.

Imagine that you have set yourself goals to lose weight or get fitter. Spending every Friday night drunk in a bar is not going to help you achieve those goals is it? Sure it is fun at the time, but you will not want to go on a run the next day for sure.

Our old friend procrastination can certainly prevent you from achieving personal goals. Putting things off all of the time because they are challenging or require effort is going to stop you achieving meaningful goals. Bad habits that distract you from your goals will also have a negative impact.

Bad Habits and Low Self Esteem

If you want to really make something of your life then having low self esteem will be a major barrier for you. Thinking that you are not a worthy person will definitely hold you back. Your bad habits can really drive down your self esteem to the point where you become depressed and cannot be bothered to do anything.

Some people are habitually late for everything. They are late for work, later for social engagements and so on. This is a path that will only lead to disaster. If you are consistently late for work then there is a very good chance that you will be fired. If you keep letting your friends down by being late they will stop inviting you to social events.

Irrational fears are bad habits. If you have a fear of public speaking for example this can cause you to have low self esteem. You feel that you are useless because you are fearful of standing up and speaking in front of others. There are a lot of bad habits that can lower your self esteem.

Bad Habits can make you Stressed

Are you in debt? Do you have a spending habit that has resulted in high levels of credit card debt? There are many people in this situation. They cannot resist buying things that they really don't need. Their homes are cluttered with things that they have hardly ever used. Financial problems can really stress people out.

How do you feel when you look in the mirror? Does the shape of your body stress you out? The reason that you are overweight and out of shape is because of your bad habits or not having good habits to prevent this.

In the next chapter we will explain how you can identify the bad habits that you need to break...

CHAPTER 2

IDENTIFYING YOUR BAD (AND GOOD) HABITS

If you want to break your bad habits then you need to know what they are. You may think that this is obvious but it isn't always. You can't change something if you are not aware of it so in this chapter we will show you how to identify your bad habits, and your good ones, so that you can move forward.

One of the most important things that you need to do is to accept that you have some bad habits. Some people find this difficult to accept for a variety of reasons but you must do it or you will not get the most from this guide.

People often do things habitually that they do not realize are bad. Sitting in front of the TV every night might not seem like a bad thing to do but human beings were designed to be active and move around a lot.

Maybe you like to eat out several times a week. Nothing wrong with that if you can afford it right? Well you may not be eating too healthily by doing this and you could certainly put the money that you are spending eating out to better use.

Some of your bad habits are going to be pretty easy to break because they don't mean that much to you. Others are going to be a lot tougher to break but when you use the techniques revealed in this guide then you will be able to break them for sure.

OK now that you have taken that first giant step of admitting that you have some bad habits let's move on...

Bad Habits get Easier

Here is something that you must understand – starting a bad habit can be really pleasurable and over time they will get easier. What do we mean by that? Well let's say that one of your bad habits is lying to your spouse.

This may have been pretty difficult for you to do at first but the more that you did it the easier it became. In the back of your mind you knew that lying to the person that you love the most in the world was the wrong thing to do but you found ways to rationalize and justify your actions. This became addictive to you.

An Effective Way to Identify Bad Habits

Go to a place where you will not be disturbed and take some paper and a pen with you. You don't want any distractions while you are doing this so put your phone in silent mode and turn off the TV. OK ask yourself this question:

"What are my bad habits?"

Is it really that simple? Yes it is if you are committed to identifying your bad habits and breaking them to move forward in your life. You need to focus on the question and write down all of the answers you receive. Your subconscious mind will provide you with the answers.

It doesn't matter what answers you receive, write them all down. Here are some examples of the kind of answers you may receive:

"I am lazy"

"I shout at my kids a lot"

"I never finish what I start"

"I am too much of a perfectionist"

"I am a procrastinator"

"I lie to my spouse"

"I spend too much money on things I don't need"

"I waste a lot of time on social media"

"I am a smoker"

"I am a drinker"

If you have a long list of bad habits then don't worry you can break them all. Not receiving answers to the question is more concerning. Just focus on the question and keep asking yourself. Something will definitely turn up!

Get Specific about your Bad Habits

Once you have your list of bad habits then you will need to be more specific about them. Ask yourself these questions and write down your answers:

- How much time do you spend indulging in each bad habit?
- How long have you indulged in each bad habit?
- How much money is each bad habit costing you?
- Does the bad habit affect your health and wellbeing?
- Does the bad habit affect your emotional health?
- Does the bad habit prevent you from doing things that you really want to do?

It is very important that you identify the negative things about all of your bad habits. You will use these later to create positive reasons why you need to break your bad habits. So keep working at this until you have a comprehensive list of bad habits and all of the specifics.

What are your Good Habits?

This is often more difficult for people to identify but it is an important thing for you to do. This will help to reinforce future good habits that you want to form. So to identify them use the same process as before but this time ask yourself:

"What are my good habits?"

Here are some examples of the answers you may receive:

"I always help people"

"I am a doer and an action taker"

"I am organized"

"I take responsibility for things"

"I am always learning new things"

When you have finished writing down your good habits go through each one and think about how they make you feel. Write your feelings down alongside each good habit. So for example if one of your answers is "I am always willing to help people" then write down the satisfaction that you get from doing this.

So now you have a list of your good and bad habits you can really start to make good progress. It wasn't that difficult was it? In the next chapter we will look at how habits actually work...

HOW HABITS ACTUALLY WORK

After identifying all of your bad habits it is natural for you to be eager to break them all quickly. But you need to be patient when it comes to breaking habits and forming new ones. There is no quick fix for this no matter what anyone tells you. Some methods work faster than others do though.

It is going to take time to break a habit and form a new one. The simplest way to define a habit is:

"A pattern of behavior formed by regular repetition – it is an acquired mode of behavior".

Let's dive a little deeper into this statement...

Pattern of Behavior

Habits are something that you do on autopilot but they all have patterns to them. A good habit is driving a car safely. When you first learned to drive you had to pay attention to everything and it was probably pretty stressful for you. Once you learned to drive you do everything automatically and just concentrate on the road.

But it is not really automatic. You are just following patterns of behavior that you have learned and perfected. It all happens very quickly so you could be forgiven for thinking that it is automatic. This is important to understand because it means that you can always break a habit.

Regular Repetition

This is a strong clue that it takes an amount of time to form a habit. You need to do it regularly and repeat the process. This actually takes effort in the beginning and you will need to apply effort when you form new empowering habits.

Acquired Mode of Behavior

A bad (or good) habit didn't just turn up in your life one day. You had to acquire it. You made a conscious decision that you wanted to create the habit and then you put time and effort into it. Every habit starts somewhere. You had to learn how to implement the habit. Some are easier to learn than others.

There is no Singular Formula for Habit Formation

Everyone is different. If you are someone that is naturally active then going to the gym on a regular basis will be an easier habit for you to form than someone who is not inclined to do this. If you have led a sedentary lifestyle for a long time then it will be much more of a challenge for you to form a "going to the gym" habit.

Different habits require different approaches. If you want to quit smoking for example, then this will require a very different approach to wanting to go to the gym three times a week. There is no single formula for habit formation. Don't believe anyone that tells you that there is.

There is a Habit Framework

Please don't think at this point that it is going to be too complicated for you to break bad habits and form new good ones. There is a framework that you can use for new habits that will work every time for you. This framework has three parts and these form a neurological loop in your mind. They are:

- Remind
- Routine
- Reward

Researchers at MIT (Massachusetts Institute of Technology) discovered the "3 R's Loop". Their research showed that these three elements were essential in the cycle for habit formation. It is important for you to grasp this as it will not only help with the formation of new good habits but also with the breaking of existing bad habits.

We will discuss this in more detail in the next chapter.

Your Habits Define you

Here is something that you must know – your habits define who you are. The routines that you run every day of your life are responsible for what you do and how productive you are and will be responsible for how you run your life and even your happiness.

So the key question is – are you in control of your habits or do they control you? The answer to this is "both". You can always control your habits – this is what this guide is all about. But remember that habits are powerful and once you establish them as part of your every day routine then you will execute them on autopilot.

Your habits become a part of you and if you are not careful they can control your life. If you have an alcohol or drug habit then this can soon become an addiction that spirals your life out of control. It will take some serious commitment and effort to break a habit like this. But the good news is that it is possible.

You want Good Habits to Control you

If a habit is doing you good then you want it to control you. People often become anxious about something controlling them but this is not always a bad thing. If you have a habit of exercising regularly then it is good to be controlled by this.

The same goes for cleaning your home every week, always finishing the things that you start, bathing every day and cleaning your teeth morning and night. There are some habits that you need to be happy about having control over you.

In the next chapter we will take a detailed look at the habit formation process and breaking bad habits…

CHAPTER 4

HABIT FORMATION AND BREAKING BAD HABITS

We want to begin this chapter by letting you know this:

Forming a habit is not an easy thing to do!

There are a number of different factors which affect your ability to break a bad habit or form a new good one.

Time and Patience

To break a bad habit or create a new good habit requires time and patience. You may have read that there is a 21 day habit formation rule. Many self help gurus swear by this and will tell you that this is the standard amount of time to break or form a habit.

But the 21 day rule is only part of the equation. In general it takes at least 21 days for people to feel comfortable about breaking a bad habit or forming a new one. This is the minimum time for individuals to become accustomed to the changes they have made in their life.

For the breaking of a bad habit, or formation of a new one, to stick it will take longer. The psychologists will tell you that it takes an average of 66 days. When you think about it, this is not a great deal of time in the grand scheme of things (just over 2 months). But when you are just starting out this can seem like a long time.

There was an important study conducted at the University College in London where 96 people who wanted to create new habits were observed for 12 weeks. The main findings of the study were:

- It took 66 days on average for new routines to become habits
- The real numbers ranged from 18 days to 254 days

- During the study some participants failed to perform their routines every day – this did not prevent them from forming the habit in the long run

What all of this tells you is that it is probably going to take you longer than 21 days to form a new habit or break a bad one. It also tells you that if you miss a day here and there then it is not the end of the world. So we recommend that you keep doing your new routines for at least 66 days and longer if you need it.

The 3 R's Loop

Do you remember in the last chapter we talked about the 3 R's Loop? The clever people over at MIT discovered that there is a neurological loop that affects the routines that we perform regularly. Just to remind you of the three R's:

- Remind
- Routine
- Reward

Why is this a loop? Well you trigger a habit through a reminder and this will affect your routine and in turn you will feel a sense of reward from this. To look at it another way:

Remind – this is the trigger that initiates the behavior or action

Routine – this is the action or behavior

Reward – this is the pleasure or fulfillment that you get from the action or behavior

It is really important that you understand and remember the 3 R's for breaking bad habits and creating new good ones. The reason for this is that you are only going to break a bad habit if you are aware of why you keep doing it. For new habits you need to understand what will trigger it and what reward you will derive from it.

Here is an example of the 3 R's in action:

- Remind – something tells you that it is time for you to drink a beer. This can be the time of day for example.
- Routine – this is you drinking the beer
- Reward – this is the satisfying feeling that you get from drinking the beer.

Time for another beer? If the reward that you get is very pleasurable and you see it as possible then you are more likely to repeat this process. Once you start drinking beer and enjoying it, in a very short time it can become a habit if you do it often enough. For example 7pm each day is beer time so you go to the bar.

Breaking Bad Habits

OK so now you know how the 3 R's work it is time for you to use the principle to break your bad habits. There are three steps in this process:

1. Identify the Habit

We already covered this in chapter 2. The habit is the routine so let's use an example here of procrastination. Now that we have established procrastination as the habit you want to break you have to know what triggers your procrastination (the reminder). Then you need to identify the reward you get from procrastinating.

How do you do this?

Well the best way is to ask yourself questions. So to identify the trigger for your procrastination you could ask yourself:

- Why do I want to procrastinate?
- Is it because I feel overwhelmed?
- Does it provide an escape for me?

Now move on to the rewards of procrastination:

- Does it make me relaxed?
- Does it make the stress go away?
- Does it allow me to do the things that I want to do?

These questions are just examples. Ask yourself the questions that are right for you. Once you ask the right questions you will identify the triggers that remind you to procrastinate and the rewards that reinforce your procrastination habit.

2. Consider the Rewards

The rewards that you experience from your bad habits will reinforce them. So if procrastinating provides you with a relaxing escape and prevent you from becoming overwhelmed.

You do not want to be overwhelmed so whenever you are faced with a task that you are not sure how to proceed with or is really challenging then it is likely that your procrastination habit will kick in.

Now consider other things that can prevent overwhelm and provide you with an escape. What if you were to break down a large task into smaller parts so that it doesn't overwhelm you? Or perhaps you can give yourself a reward for finishing the task that relaxes you? These are good alternatives to procrastinating.

In this step you want to play around with the rewards until you find the real thing that is driving your behavior. By examining alternatives to the procrastination habit it will be possible for you to identify what the most important reward is for your procrastination. This reward is making you crave the habit of procrastination.

We gave you two alternatives to achieve the rewards. To provide you with the reward of avoiding overwhelm you can break up the task. For the reward of escaping you could choose something else that enables you to escape such as watching an entertaining video online once you have completed the task.

So think about some alternative routines and write down how you feel about these alternatives. By doing this you gain a better understanding of your actions and emotions. You can also post these alternatives as possible solutions to break your habit in the future. Remember that it will take time to eradicate your bad habits.

Now let's move to step 3.

3. Identify Reminders

OK we are not going to pull any punches here. This is the most difficult step. The reason for this is that a number of different triggers surround us. Think about your daily habit of eating your lunch. The action of eating lunch can be triggered by the time of day (for example 1pm is lunchtime).

Or you could find that your stomach starts to rumble and this triggers your lunch time. What about if you are at work and some of your colleagues tell you that it is lunchtime and they want you to go with them?

So given this how do you identify reminders? Well the best way is to specific patterns of behavior and action in relation to a number of different habit categories. These categories are the result of a number of research studies that directly affect the behavior and actions of people.

There are five categories:
1. Time of day
2. Where you are located
3. Your emotional state
4. Other people
5. The action preceding your urge

You have identified being easily distracted as a bad habit. Take a look at the table below to get a better idea of how this can be triggered:

	Day 1	Day 2	Day 3	Day 4	Day 5
Time of day	11.10am	1.43pm	9.06am	3.17pm	4.33pm
Your location	Home	Home	Office	Meeting room	Office
Emotional State	Bored	Bored	Bored	Bored	Bored
Other people	Tara	Nobody	James	Nobody	Kirsty
Preceding action	Talked to Tara on the phone	Finished eating late lunch	Received email from James	Set up room for a presentation	Sent email to Kirsty

Only one of the categories has a distinctive pattern in this case and that is your emotional state. So you can confidently conclude that when you are bored you are the most likely to be distracted. Once you have identified your main reminder you can now take the necessary steps to break your habit.

In the next chapter we will discuss how to create new good habits with the 3 R's…

FORMING NEW HABITS USING THE 3 R'S

The best way to form a new habit is to use the 3 R's neurological loop. Again this is a 3 step process like the breaking of a bad habit we discussed in the last chapter. But there are some differences. It is best to explain how this works through the use of an example:

Let's say that you eat pretty healthily but you are not getting enough exercise. You don't want to join a gym and you have the space to exercise at home. You like swimming and bike riding so you want to include this into your new routine. You want to turn all of this into a new habit.

Step 1 – Start with a Reminder

You are aware that "remind" is one of the 3 R's and an important part of the habit forming process. The reminder is the trigger for you to perform your routine that will later become the new habit. Reminders need to be strong and not based on memory or will power as these are not reliable.

What a lot of people will do is to create a daily plan over the next week or two for their new habit. The plan is written in the form of a list that the individual carries around with them. They believe that this is a good enough reminder to take action.

While a list like this might work for some people it is unlikely to work for everyone. If for some reason you forget to do something on the list one day then this can compromise the whole thing. People often get caught up in other things and forget. You cannot always rely on willpower either.

Here is a better method. Take a piece of paper and divide it into 2 columns. In the top left write the heading "Existing Habits" and in the top right "Daily Recurrences". Write in the left hand column all the things that you always do each day. In the right column write the things that happen in your life each day that you don't have control of:

Existing Habits	Daily Recurrences
Bathe	Neighbors play loud music
Clean your teeth	Traffic on the way to work
Get dressed	Manager's review meeting
Eat breakfast	
Wash the dishes	
Make dinner	

To create a strong reminder you want to associate it with an item on the list that you are in control of. So for example when you "get dressed" you can lay out your clothes for your exercise session. By setting a reminder in this way you never have to rely on remembering or willpower. You are always going to get dressed in the morning.

Now you need a new routine.

Step 2 – Make a New Easy Routine

It is important that you do not make your new exercise routine too complicated to begin with. If you do this then it will be a lot more likely that you fail and procrastinate over your new routine. So start off with some gentle stretching exercises that you can do when you wake up in the morning for example.

You can add some simple exercises to this that you can easily do at home such as planks, lunges, dips etc. These will help you to build up your strength and endurance preparing you for more intense workouts later on.

Tweak this until you get it right. If you set an exercise routine that is too tough for you each day then tone it down. Conversely if it is too easy then take it up a notch. The establishment of the new routine is more important than the exercises particularly in the early stages of habit formation. So make the routine as easy as you can.

Step 3 - Use Rewards and Celebrate

Having a positive reward associated to your new routine will make it a whole lot easier to perform each day. So you need to come up with a reward system that is going to provide you with the necessary motivation to persist with your new routine.

What do you really enjoy that is simple and easy to implement? If you are on a healthy diet then you probably can't eat some of the foods that you really enjoy. What if you could have a small piece of chocolate as a reward for completing a week of your new routine for example?

Another example could be that you reward yourself with a massage or a bubble bath. You know the simple things in life that you really enjoy so think about these and decide on your reward system. The system must contain rewards that you will really look forward to so that you keep on going with your new exercise routine even when you don't feel like it.

You should create a reward system that gets better over time. So there is a simple reward for week 1, a slightly better reward for week 2 and so on. Think about the 21 day factor and the 66 day factor here and structure your reward system to celebrate these milestones.

Do not treat the reward step lightly. The best way to form a new habit is to continually repeat a new routine. So put every effort into motivating yourself to start and finish the routine each day.

In the next chapter we will look at how you can change your life for the better with the power of habits...

CHAPTER 6

CHANGE YOUR LIFE FOR THE BETTER WITH THE POWER OF HABITS

When you make a commitment to break your bad habits and form new empowering ones you will provide much needed clarity in your life. Most people find that they chase around all day doing a lot of things that are not really that important. Their schedules become easily cluttered as they just add things to it without giving it a lot of thought.

Does this sound like you?

So we recommend that you use habits as a powerful way to do the things that are really important to you in life. Obviously you still have to do those things that you need to do (at least for a while anyway) but with old bad habits eliminated and new empowering habits formed you will have more time and energy to do what you really want.

Take a look at your Priorities

In order to form the new empowering habits to change your life, the first step is to take a close look at your priorities. If you are unsure how to do this then begin by defining what your personal values are. Once you have established what these are you will find it much easier to determine your life priorities.

What kind of personal values should you have? Well here are some recommendations that you should adopt:

Be Committed to Goals

The best way to achieve the things that you really want in life is to be a goal oriented person. This means that you will continually challenge yourself by setting and achieving both short term and long term goals.

When you set your goals you will be able to work out what new behaviors you require and the actions you need to perform to achieve these goals. This will ensure that you focus on the right new habits to form and help to identify existing habits that need to go as they will prevent you from goal achievement.

Be an Action Taker

Another excellent personal value is to be an action taker. Rather than waste your time on meaningless activities you focus your actions on the achievement of your goals. We all only have so much time every day so be sure to put this to good use by taking the right action.

If you have a habit of coming home from work and turning on the TV then you need to eradicate this. The same goes for spending hours on social media. You need to keep taking action regularly and not let procrastination prevent you from getting what you want.

Be a People Person

People are a very important part of your life. They will provide you with the support that you will need to make the necessary habit transitions so that you can achieve your goals. So you want to surround yourself with the right people who will provide support to you.

This doesn't mean that it is all about you. You need to have a presence in the lives of people that mean the most to you. Being compassionate, understanding, patient and giving are fine personal qualities to have.

Discipline and Organization

You need discipline to keep on going in the pursuit of all your goals. There will be tough times where you will need all of the motivation you can muster to overcome obstacles and keep on the right path. Temptations are all around us these days, so discipline is essential for your success.

Organization is very important too. If your life is full of clutter then you need to sort this out. Get yourself organized in all aspects of your life which includes the storing of important documents and other physical things in your home and office as well as a well organized computer so that you know where everything is.

In the next chapter we will discuss the importance of a plan for your habit transition…

CHAPTER 7

PLANNING YOUR SUCCESSFUL HABIT TRANSITION

You now know how to break bad habits and form new empowering ones. The problem is that making these transitions is not an easy thing to do. You are going to be implementing a number of changes in your life and the best way to give you the most chance of success is through the creation of a plan.

Habit Formation Phases

You may not be surprised to know that there are three main phases to habit formation. These are:

1. Honeymoon phase
2. Critical phase
3. Second nature phase

These phases are not always linear (moving naturally from one to another) and sometimes you can find that you go in and out of the different phases. You need to be aware of what all of these phases mean so that you can monitor your progress effectively.

Honeymoon Phase

As the name suggests, this is the new, exciting and fun phase of habit formation. It is like when you first meet someone and fall in love. You have more zest for life and you are motivated to make any changes necessary to keep this going.

The problem with the honeymoon phase is that it only lasts for a certain period of time. At some stage reality will kick in and you will automatically enter the next phase. This is a shame, just as it is with new relationships, but it happens so you need to take this into consideration.

Critical Phase

After the honeymoon phase comes the critical phase. This is a vulnerable time as you can start to have doubts about everything just like in a relationship. You start to think whether your new exercise habit is really worth all of the trouble. Motivation is a lot weaker during this phase.

The good news is that you can survive the critical stage if you approach it properly. The first thing you need to do is to recognize that there is a problem. If your motivation is waning then remind yourself that forming a new habit is tough.

Then you need to decide whether you will carry on or not. We want you to stick to your new routine so ask yourself "How will I feel if I fail with my new routine?" Think about the great feelings you have already experienced with your new routine and make these feelings strong within you.

The final step to get through the critical phase is to visualize your life in the longer term after the routine becomes a habit. See yourself fitter and looking good if your habit is around exercise. How will you look in one year's time? What about five year's time? If you stop your routine now you will not look as good will you?

Second Nature Phase

You can probably guess what this phase is all about. When you get here your new routine(s) will feel second nature to you. They are getting closer to becoming an automatic habit. But there are a couple of things that can make you head back to the critical phase so you need to be careful.

Something may change in your life that could cause a disruption to your routine. The other thing that can happen is that you experience feelings of discouragement again like you did in the critical phase. If either of these things happen then always focus on the long term aim to provide you with the inspiration and motivation to see the habit through.

Your Habit Transition Plan

You need a good plan to enable you to keep going with your routine(s). We recommend the following 3 steps to create the best habit transition plan:

1. Create a list of your small steps and long term goals
2. Eliminate unwanted results
3. Associate desired behaviors

Let's take a look at each of these in turn.

Creating a List of your Small Steps and Long Term Goals

It is very important that you use the power of visualization to see your long term goals as a reality. This will make you much more likely to stick to your habit transitions because you will see what your life will be like in the future.

It is not always easy to visualize long term goals properly so it is important to identify smaller steps that will help you to make progress towards these longer term goals. So of your long term goal is to be physically fit and ripped then a smaller step is to perform a simple exercise routine every day for example.

The important thing with the smaller steps is that they all dovetail in to your longer term goal. By writing a list of these steps you can ensure that this happens. This is an essential step to take if you are attempting to break a number of bad habits and form new ones at the same time.

So for the fitness goal some smaller steps could be simple exercises each day, following a healthier diet, going to the gym three times a week and so on. All of these small steps make visualization easier.

Eliminate Unwanted Results

This is all about removing temptations from your path. If you want to be fit then it is not a great idea to fill your kitchen with candies or snacks that are unhealthy for example. Of course you can never completely eliminate everything. Maybe someone comes to visit and brings something delicious with them. Going off the rails occasionally is OK.

Make a list of the things that could result in you failing with your routine(s). Visualize the potential pitfalls in your journey. Remove any distractions that are likely to cause a disruption for you. Sometimes can just happen that could distract you.

If you always go for a run at a certain time each day and somebody approaches you to do something else at that same time of day then you need to see this as a potential disruptor. You need to be strong here and politely tell them that you can't do it.

Associating Desired Behaviors

This is a simple process of associating desired behaviors to things that you already do in your life. You can also use this as a way of avoiding possible disruptions. So for example if you always run at 7pm each evening and you know that your friend has a habit of turning up around that time then set out a few minutes earlier so that you can avoid this problem.

Let's say that you want to achieve two different goals at once. One of these is to be fit and the other is to learn a new skill. What you could do here is to find some audio recordings that will help you to develop your new skill and listen to this while you are exercising.

Your Morning Routine is Essential

Having a good morning routine will set the tone for your day. If you start your day off in the right way then you will have more energy and be more efficient and productive throughout the day.

Studies have shown that we only have so much willpower and this dissipates slowly as the day goes on. Each decision that we make (however small) contributes to this dissipation. So having a great morning routines will help to minimize the number of decisions that you need to make the rest of the day.

Another great reason for a good morning routine is that it provides us with a greater sense of control over our life. It can help you to minimize any anxiety due to anxiety because you know what you are going to be doing each day.

So add a good morning routine to your plan. Do things that will make you feel positive and energized first thing. Create a task list for the things that you need to achieve for the day. In this way there is no anxiety for you at the start of your day and this will make you feel very positive about the rest of it.

In the next chapter will discuss how you can reinforce new habits…

CHAPTER 8

NEW HABIT REINFORCEMENT

So far in this guide you have learned how you can break bad habits and form new good habits effectively. Once you have created a new habit it is a good idea to reinforce it. Fortunately, there are a number of different ways that you can do this.

Having taken all of the time and trouble to break a bad habit and create a new empowering one, the last thing you want is to break the new habit. So here are some good ways to prevent you from sabotaging a new habit.

Use a Physical Interrupter

If this sounds crazy then please stay with us. Before we get into how using a rubber band helps you to prevent the breaking of a new habit we want to tell you that failing to perform a habit is something that people do all of the time. This can be something that they have done for years and a good habit.

So if you always take a shower when you get up in the morning but you have woken up late and only have time for a quick wash instead then this is OK. It does not mean that you have failed as a person. It is a natural thing to happen from time to time.

How does a rubber band help with all of this? Well it is a really easy concept to grasp. Just place a rubber band around your wrist (you could use a stretch bracelet if you prefer this) and any time that you feel like breaking your new habit just snap the rubber band.

The snapping of the rubber band triggers another action that will prevent you from breaking the habit. So of you have got into the habit of exercising every day and then suddenly you don't feel like exercising just snap the band to focus back to the good habit.

When using the rubber band method to reinforce a new habit you need to prepare an alternative behavior or action to follow so that you can stay on track. The snapping of the band forces you to be more aware of your thoughts, actions and behaviors. It is a physical reminder that has better impact than a thought.

Keep wearing the rubber band and snapping it until you no longer need to do this. There will come a time when you are much more aware of your thoughts, actions and behaviors and no longer require it.

Make a Change to your Environment

This is all about avoiding the triggers that prevented you from doing the right things prior to forming the new habit. A lot of these triggers will still exist in your environment so where you can make changes to your surroundings.

So for example, if your friend always calls around to see you when you want to take your daily run, talk to them and arrange for them to come at a later time. Or maybe your running route takes you through an area where some of your friends live who always try and stop you running then choose a different route.

Spice up your Reward System

We strongly recommend the use of a reward system to create all of your new habits. Over time your reward system may lose its appeal and not motivate you as much as it used to. If this happens then it is time for you to rethink your current reward system.

So if a nice bubble bath was the reward for exercising every day for a week and this does not excite you any more then come up with something new such as a trip to the shops or an evening watching a movie with your family.

Make a Wager with someone

You can make a wager (a bet) with someone that you know and trust that you will stick to your new habit. The wager needs to be high enough so that it will really hurt you if you fail. This will provide you with more accountability for your actions and act as a strong deterrent to giving up on your new habit.

How much you are prepared to wager is up to you. Only you know what is going to be really painful for you. You don't have to use money – you can make the wager around losing something that is really precious to you such as a piece of jewelry or a set of golf clubs. Just ensure that the pain will be really intense if you lose the wager.

In the next chapter we will discuss empowering habits that you should live by...

CHAPTER 9

EMPOWERING HABITS YOU SHOULD LIVE BY

Now you are all set to break your bad habits and form empowering new habits. If you are finding it difficult choosing which new habits you should form in your life then we have 7 ideas for you in this chapter.

1. Establish an Empowering Morning Routine

We have discussed the benefits of a good morning routine already. Now it is time to make it happen. It is essential that you get a great start to each day so think about the things that you can do when you first get up to achieve this.

Doing some gentle stretching and breathing exercises is certainly a good thing to do. You can find examples of these online and they will not take you very long. A few minutes spent in the morning doing this will get your heart pumping and improve your circulation.

Creating a plan for the day is another good idea. Take a few minutes first thing to write down the things that you want to do. This will help avoid uncertainty and anxiety. Write some positive affirmations that you can read out aloud every morning to put you into a positive frame of mind.

2. Exercise every Day

This is an excellent habit to live by. When you exercise just a few minutes each day you will improve your health and wellbeing. It will help you to fight off health problems such as high blood pressure and heart disease.

After exercising you will feel great because you will release those "feel good" endorphins into your system. Regular exercise also helps you to develop your strength and endurance so that you can tackle anything that comes your way.

3. Do not relate Happiness to things out of your control

There are so many people that let things that are out of their control dictate whether they are happy or not. The economy has taken a nose dive so they go around moping all day long. It is raining outside and they are only happy when the sun is shining.

Closer to home do not tie your happiness with that of your spouse. A lot of people do this. If your spouse is feeling down for some reason then you automatically feel down. You need to find things that make you happy independently of things that you cannot control.

You are always going to have bad days – we all do. Learn how to bounce back from anything that has made you unhappy. It is OK to be sad and upset for a short period of time but you need to break out of this as soon as possible.

4. Don't waste Money on Pointless Possessions

Are you someone that likes to buy a lot of possessions? If you are then consider this – possessions lose their flavor pretty quickly. How often have you been excited about buying something and then when you got it quickly losing interest in it?

Get into the habit of spending money on experiences instead. An experience will inspire you a lot more than a possession will. Experiences form part of who you are and will help you to become a better person. Your experiences are unique to you and are much more likely to make you happy.

5. Get into the Grateful Habit

Being grateful for what you already have is a great way to live. We recommend that you start a gratitude journal and write down 3 things that you are grateful for each day. It is a good idea to add this to your morning routine.

Gratitude is not just about things. You can, and should, be grateful for the people in your life and the things that they do for you. You can be grateful for the fact that you have good health and that you have the money to put food on the table etc. Living a life of gratitude will bring you more than you can ever have imagined.

6. Be Spontaneous sometimes

This may surprise you as habit formation is all about routines and consistency. But don't ignore an itch to do something now and again. Spontaneity is good for you now and again and helps to make life interesting. Find happiness in surprises that you experience.

7. Live by a Budget

Are you in control of your money? Most people are not. A great habit to develop is a budgeting one. Look at all of your expenditure and cut out what isn't necessary. Then create a budget around your essential outgoings, your financial plans for the future and your fun money.

Essential outgoings will include things like the electric and gas bills, telephone bills, Internet access, groceries, car payments and so on. Determine a percentage of your income to save every month for your future. Work out what is left for "fun money" or flexible spending. If this is not enough then look at ways to increase your income.

In the last chapter we will look at the best practices for breaking bad habits and forming new ones...

BEST PRACTICES

Here are the X best practices that we strongly recommend that you follow to break your bad habits and form new good habits that will change your life for the better. It is not easy to break bad habits or form new ones but the end result will certainly be worth it for you so embrace these best practices and create the life that you want.

1. Have a Strong Reason

When you are doing something really challenging that requires a lot of time, effort and persistence like breaking a bad habit or forming a new habit then you need a strong reason (why) to keep you motivated. Write your reason down and attach strong feelings to it. Be sure to carry this around with you at all times.

2. Identify your Habits

Some of your good and bad habits will be obvious but some won't. When you want to get rid of your bad habits then you need to identify them first if you don't know what they all are. Go to a quiet place with a pen and paper and ask yourself the question "what are my bad habits?" Your subconscious will tell you and you must write them down.

3. Understand how Habits work

It will be a lot easier for you to break bad habits and form new ones if you know how habits work. Make sure that you understand the 3 R's which are Reminder, Routine and Reward. A habit is a neurological loop of the 3 R's. The reminder triggers the habit, the routine is the behavior or action and the reward is the feeling you experience during and after the habit.

4. Breaking Bad Habits

It is not easy to break a habit especially if you have had it for a number of years. Forming a new habit is difficult as well. Some experts will tell you that it takes just 21 days to break a habit or form a new one but this is not the case. In 21 days you should feel comfortable with the change that you have made. It will take an average of 66 days to form an automatic habit.

You can break habits using the 3 R's. The first step is to identify the habit and then find out what rewards you get from it by asking yourself questions. Now find another positive routine which will provide you with the same reward. The final step is to identify triggers for the bad habit so that you can use your new positive routine instead.

5. Forming New Habits

To form a new habit you will use the 3 R's neurological loop again. There is a 3 step process to form a new habit. The first step is to come up with a trigger or "reminder" for the new habit. The most effective way to do this is to link the trigger to something that you do every day already such as brushing your teeth or getting dressed.

Step 2 is the introduction of an easy routine which will eventually become the new habit. Don't make the mistake of trying to do too much here because it will be difficult to sustain. The final step is to decide on a reward for your new habit and celebrate the achievement of milestones often.

6. Personal Values

Take a look at your priorities before you form any new habits. Look at your personal values for ideas for new habits. We recommend that you have 4 personal values that will prepare you for a life changing transformation.

The four personal values are 1) A commitment to goal setting and achieving goals, 2) Being an action taker, 3) Being a people person and 4) being disciplined and organized. If you do not have any of these personal values then we strongly recommend that you adopt them and form new goals around them.

7. Habit Formation Phases

There are three phases to habit formation that you need to be aware of. These are 1) Honeymoon phase, 2) Critical phase and 3) Second nature phase. When you first start with your new habit you are very excited about it and will do anything to form the new habit. It is similar to falling in love with someone.

This is the honeymoon phase which unfortunately doesn't always last that long. Reality kicks in and you start to question why you are working so hard to form this new habit (similar to questioning whether you have chosen the right partner or not). You have now entered the critical phase and you must survive this if you are to form your habit.

Think about the big picture when you are in the critical stage. Visualize to see what the new habit will mean to you in the future and experience the great feelings it will give you. The final stage is the second nature phase where you continue with the new routine as if it was "second nature".

8. Reinforce New Habits

Even when you have gone past the 66 day mark you will still need to reinforce your new habit in the early stages. Using a physical interrupter like a rubber band around your wrist is a good idea. If you ever feel like breaking the new habit then snap the band against your wrist.

There are other techniques for reinforcement that you can use as well. Some of the best ones are making changes to your environment to avoid previous triggers, changing up your reward system and making a wager with someone that you will stick with your new habit.

9. Live by these Habits

We strongly recommend that you live by these 7 habits:

1. An empowering morning routine
2. Exercise daily
3. Don't relate your happiness to things outside of your control
4. Don't waste money on pointless possessions
5. Be grateful
6. Be spontaneous
7. Live by a budget

If you need ideas for the formation of new habits then look at this list for inspiration. No matter where you are in your life these are great habits to live by.

CONCLUSION

We have worked hard to bring you everything that you need to break your bad habits and form new empowering habits in your life. Please do not just read this guide and then do nothing. Take the time to identify your bad habits, decide on new good habits and make these important changes in your life.

A lot of people want to change their lives for the better. They do not realize that their habits define their life and where they are going. So make a commitment to get rid of those habits which are preventing you from having the things that you want in your life and forming new habits which will enable you to achieve your goals.

The next move is yours. We have provided you with compelling reasons why you need to change your habits and given you all of the tools that you need to do this in the most effective way. So take action right now and prepare to change your life for the better.

We wish you every success with your new habits!

Breaking Bad Habits – Cheat Sheet

Proven Ways To Build Good Habits And Break Bad Ones

Step 1: Why you need to break Bad Habits

- Your choices have a dramatic effect on your life
- It can save you time
- Improve your relationships
- Help you to achieve your goals
- Improve your self esteem
- Reduce your stress

Step 2: Identify your Habits

Step #1: Most people do not know all of their habits

Step #2: Realize that habits get easier over time

Step #3: Go to a quiet place with a pen and paper

Step #4: Ask yourself what your bad habits are

Step #5: Your subconscious mind will provide the answers

Step #6: Write everything down

Step #7: Get specific with your habits

Step 3: How Habits work

- Pattern of behavior formed by regular repetition
- It is not really automatic
- Habits strengthen over time
- You acquired all your habits
- 3 R's Neurological Loop

- Reminder
- Routine
- Reward

Step 4: Breaking Bad Habits

Step #1: Understand it takes time and patience

Step #2: 21 days to be comfortable with new routine

Step #3: 66 days to make the new routine a habit

Step #4: Use the 3 R's

Step #5: Identify the habit

Step #6: Consider the rewards

Step #7: Use a new routine to provide the same reward

Step #8: Identify the reminders

Step 5: Forming New Habits

Step #1: Use the 3 R's

Step #2: Start with a reminder

Step #3: Reminder associated with what you do now

Step #4: Create an easy routine

Step #5: Don't try to do too much

Step #6: Use rewards and celebrate

Step 6: Change your life with Habits

Step #1: Take a look at your priorities

Step #2: What are your personal values?

Step #3: Be committed to goals

Step #4: Be an action taker

Step #5: Be a people person

Step #6: Be disciplined and organized

Step 7: Habit Formation Phases

Step #1: You need to plan your habit formations

Step #2: Three phases you need to be aware of

Step #3: Honeymoon phase

Step #4: Critical phase

Step #5: Second nature phase

Step #6: It is possible to move between different phases

Step 8: New Habit Reinforcement

Step #1: You can be tempted to break a habit

Step #2: Use a rubber band on your wrist

Step #3: Make changes to your environment

Step #4: Spice up your reward system

Step #5: Place a wager with someone

Step 9: Empowering Habits to live by

Step #1: Empowering morning routine

Step #2: Exercise every day

Step #3: Happiness not related to things you can't control

Step #4: Don't waste money on pointless possessions

Step #5: Gratitude

Step #6: Be spontaneous sometimes

Step #7: Live by a budget

Step 10: Habits Best Practices

- Have a strong reason

- Identify your habits

- Understand how habits work

- Break bad habits

- Form new good habits

- Personal Values

- Navigate habit formation phases

- Reinforce new habits

- 7 habits to live by

Breaking Bad Habits – Resources Report

Resource #1

Look for other examples of why you should change bad habits and form new good ones

Research case studies online of how people have transformed their lives for the better by changing their habits

Look online for examples of people failing with breaking their bad habits and identify why they failed. Do the same for new habits.

Goal: Prepare yourself for breaking your bad habits and forming new empowering habits to change your life for the better

Resource #2

Look for psychological studies that show how habits work to enhance your knowledge

Search online for the MIT research about the 3 R's of habit formation

Find research studies that support the premise of the 21 day rule for becoming accustomed to new routines

Find research evidence that supports the notion of the 66 day average duration for new habit formation

Goal: Find out as much as you can about how habits really work. Pay close attention to the 3 R's and how they form the neurological loop. Learn how the 21 day and 66 day rules came into being.

Resource #3

Look online for alternative ways to identify habit triggers

Look online for examples of new routines that you can implement to provide the same rewards as your bad habits

Look online for examples of reward systems that you can implement for the forming of new habits

Goal: Prepare yourself fully for the breaking of bad habits and the formation of new empowering habits.

Resource #4

Look for examples online of good habits that you can form to assist with your goal setting and achievement

Look for examples online of good habits you can form to make you take more action

Look for examples online of good habits you can form to improve your social skills

Look for examples online of good habits you can form to make you more disciplined and organized

Goal: Do your homework and make sure that you form the best new habits that will help you to get where you want to be in your life.

Resource #5

Look for other examples online of how to navigate through the critical stage of habit formation

Find other methods online of how you can reinforce your new habits

Goal: Once you make the commitment to form a new habit you must get through the critical phase to make it stick and then use methods to reinforce the habit once it is in place.

CPSIA information can be obtained
at www.ICGtesting.com
Printed in the USA
BVHW011050050321
601707BV00024B/153